Bloomberg
New Contemporaries 2011

Selectors:
Pablo Bronstein, Sarah Jones and Michael Raedecker

Bloomberg first sponsored New Contemporaries in 1999, creating a dynamic partnership that has provided a vital platform for over 450 of the UK's most exciting emerging artists.

As a company with an international reputation for supporting new ideas and extraordinary talent, our long-term partnership with New Contemporaries reflects our ongoing philanthropic commitment to contemporary arts initiatives that put innovation and access at their core.

Bloomberg is a global financial information and news provider that connects influential decision makers to a dynamic network of information, people and ideas. For this reason, we are particularly proud to help so many recent graduates and fine art students from the UK access the vital networks and opportunities they need to build national and international careers as a direct result of New Contemporaries.

Now supporting many New Contemporaries alumni through our extensive programme of contemporary arts sponsorship around the world, we are excited to see another 40 young artists gain the wider recognition and skills they need to take their work to new audiences around the UK.

Bloomberg

Foreword

I truly am thrilled with the selectors: Pablo Bronstein, Sarah Jones and Michael Raedecker. They all gave so much to the daunting task of starting from the enormous pool of submissions, honing the work down, arguing fairly with perception, yet maintaining separate voices whilst listening to each other. They showed real insight and a desire for work to shine out, to function in its own terms.

I am particularly excited by the selection, by the work and therefore by the artists who will be part of Bloomberg New Contemporaries 2011. We are to show first in Sheffield at S1 Artspace and at Site Gallery and then in London at the ICA for the second subsequent year. Both locations will bring something different out of this very strong work.

To some extent this year's catalogue continues to extend the selection with writing on individual pieces, by including short texts written by a number of past Bloomberg New Contemporaries artists. This is to reinforce the strong peer structure that inevitably builds up around the exhibition, an involvement that can debunk any spurious mystery about the authority of selection and can show that writing about art and making art are wholly intertwined. We have also commissioned an essay by Peter Osborne, the well-known teacher of philosophy who has long engaged with visual art, who has addressed the notion of the contemporary in a fascinating text that runs parallel to and perhaps cuts across or questions our annual desire to celebrate the very best art of the time.

Bloomberg New Contemporaries is rare – even rarer in this climate – in that it arrives out of an open submission and there is no pre-selection. Such a thing is of primary importance: it is totally democratic and goes against the grain of cronyism and collective assumption. The opportunity to develop, encourage and cherish the relationship between artists in New Contemporaries over the years is very special.

I continue to feel eternally grateful and confident in the fantastic level of support and loyalty shown to us by both the Arts Council and Bloomberg, both of which have committed to working with us in the coming years.

Sacha Craddock
Chair of the Board of Directors of Bloomberg New Contemporaries

Look Beneath the Label:
Notes on the Contemporary

Peter Osborne

'This is so contemporary, contemporary, contemporary!
This so contemporary.'

This is So Contemporary, Tino Sehgal, 2003

Claims to be contemporary can readily provoke ridicule, especially
in art, but they are unavoidable nonetheless. Quite why this has
become so, and what it means for current art practices, is something
of an enigma. On the one hand, it seems obvious: if 'contemporary' has
come to mean up-to-the-minute – the latest thing – and art continues to
legitimate itself as a cultural carrier of 'the new', then it is not surprising
that it has become one of art's basic functions to be contemporary, in
the sense of *sharing the time* of the most recent, the most 'actual' things,
articulating a sense of a living present. (After all, didn't the US art critic
Michael Fried famously claim that 'presentness is grace', as long ago
as the mid-1960s – although he didn't mean it in quite this sense.) This
may leave art prey to the logic of fashion, and the ridiculousness that on
occasion accompanies the pursuit of stylistic difference. But if art is not
prepared to run the risk of ridiculousness, what chance has it of being
decisively different or significantly new?

On the other hand, however, matters are a little more complicated
and obscure. Can the contemporary really be reduced to a felt quality
of up-to-dateness? And if not, what exactly is involved in the claim of
art to be contemporary?

Tino Sehgal's 2003 performance piece for gallery attendants,
This is So Contemporary, is subtly indicative of the concealed depth
of the waters here. For while the deflationary humour of its chanted
self-assertion of contemporaneity throws a harsh light on the pretensions
of whatever is being shown in the space where it is performed, it also
acts as a protective coat of irony for more serious claims, implicit in
its self-referential structure: about the contemporaneity of performance
(in distinction from object-based practices, for example) and ultimately
about the performative character of all art. Tautological, parodical and
polemical at the same time, the piece lays bare the blanket demand
for contemporaneity imposed by the institutional spaces of art.

In doing so, it reminds us of two things. One is that the contemporary
is a critical, selective concept. To claim something is contemporary
is to make a claim for its significance in showing us something about
the quality of the present – a claim over and against those of some
other things, some of which themselves may make the same claim
to be contemporary. The other is that this present is a shared present,

a coming together of the times of different lives (artists and audiences, for example), against which such claims must be judged.

The basic idea of the contemporary as a 'living, existing or occurring together' has been around a long time. Derived from the medieval Latin *contemporarius*, and the late Latin *contemporalis*, the English 'contemporary' dates from around the mid-seventeenth century. It was only after the Second World War, however, that it began to acquire its current critical connotations through its use, first, as a specification of, and then in contrast to, periodising uses of 'modern'. Perhaps it was the collective sense of survival in the aftermath of a war that had opened up social experience beyond national frontiers, which produced the association of the new historical period with the quality of the shared present itself. The immediate postwar years saw new uses of 'contemporary' to denote both a specific style of design ('contemporary design') and the arts of the present more generally ('contemporary arts'), in their differences from those of the preceding period. This is the historical source of the sense of up-to-dateness with which the term is increasingly identified in popular usage.

In Great Britain, when the Institute of Contemporary Arts was founded in London in 1946 – as one of the first organisations to consciously identify with presenting the 'contemporary' – it was very up-to-date indeed. Doubly and paradoxically so, in so far as it both fed off the residual energies of the avant-garde, acting out a less forceful version of its temporal logic of futurity, and took a step back from that futurity into a more expansive present. Modern, avant-garde, contemporary: two steps forward, one step back. It transformed 'advanced' art's identification with a radically different future (associated in Britain with Surrealism) into identification with a more extended present. This present was marked not by the anticipation of an end of art (the famous avant-garde dissolution of art into life) but by interactions between the arts – including popular and technologically advanced arts, like cinema, advertising and the comic strip, in particular; arts that were largely unrecognised by institutions like the Royal Academy of Arts. (Some things have not changed so much.) However, the separating out of 'modern' and 'contemporary' that this notion of contemporary arts anticipated in no way dominated the institutional field of art at that time. There, the contemporary acted as a qualification of (rather than a counter to) 'the modern': the contemporary was the most recent modern, but a modern with a waning futurity.

'Contemporary' still wasn't enough of a critical concept in its own right in the 1970s to make it into Raymond Williams's influential *Keywords: A Vocabulary of Culture and Society* (1976). And when, a decade later, Matei Calinescu updated his book *Faces of Modernity* into *Five Faces of Modernity* (1987) it was 'Postmodernism' that provided the topic for the new chapter (alongside 'Modernism', 'avant-garde', 'decadence' and 'kitsch'). In fact, it has been only with the decisive discrediting of Postmodernism as a coherent critical concept over the last decade, that 'contemporary' has begun to emerge into the critical daylight from beneath its function as a label denoting what is current or up-to-date. Hence the recent rush of writing trying to make some minimal critical sense of the concept.[1] This throws the founding of New Contemporaries, in 1988,[2] into an interesting light, retrospectively. The 'new' in its title functions as a marker both of the need to intensify the standard sense of contemporary with a greater urgency, and of an acknowledgement that the culturally dominant trope through which to achieve such urgency remains the repetition of 'the new': the metronome of the modern produces the contemporary anew.

Enveloped within the periodicity of the human lifespan, 'contemporary' is at base a generational term. But in modernity's subjection of the time of generations to the destruction of tradition, its duration has fractured into ever shorter periods, retreating to the main mediating form between what philosophers call 'physical' or 'cosmological' time, on the one hand, and 'social' time on the other: the calendar year. New Contemporaries offers us new contemporaries, each year. For all the rhetoric of the machine, the rhythm of the new continues to find its measure in the seasonal rhythm of the annual. Generations become graduations. In this respect, New Contemporaries is the Beaujolais Nouveau of British art schools, the latest batch: fresh, raw, exercises in art. (No bad way to pass a week in November; but whose cellar is hiding the *en primeur*?) 'Contemporary' is suspended here somewhere between a name and a concept, a fact and a hope. It simultaneously evokes and suspends the increasingly insistent critical claim with which the word is now associated.

At its deepest, the concept of the contemporary engages that most basic of issues: the framework of critical judgement of art, at the point of its crisis. In the heyday of formalist-modernist criticism (from the late 1940s to the mid-1960s), the framework of criticism was set by the concept of medium. US critic Clement Greenberg appropriated the 'arts' to 'mediums' (practices to their results) and propounded a critical theory of the historical developments of mediums: purification through self-criticism, or progressive reduction to what is 'essential' to each medium. Individual works were judged in the context of this narrative. This framework was set against a whole other modernist tradition

1. See Terry Smith, 'Contemporary Art and Contemporaneity', *Critical Inquiry* 32, Summer 2006, pp. 681–707; Giorgi Agamben, 'What is the Contemporary?', in his *What is an Apparatus? and Other Essays*, Stanford University Press, Stanford, 2009, pp. 39–54; John Rajchman, 'The Contemporary: A New Idea?', in Armen Avanessian and Luke Skrebowski (eds), *Aesthetics and Contemporary Art*, Sternberg Press, Berlin and New York, 2011, pp. 125–144, and in the same volume, my own 'The Fiction of the Contemporary', *Aesthetics and Contemporary Art*, op. cit., pp. 101–123.

2. The annual exhibition was first set up in 1949 and was known as Young Contemporaries. In 1987 the Arts Council of Great Britain commissioned a feasibility report to look into the future viability of the exhibition. The report was published in 1988 and a new constitution and new structure for the organisation was established, which became known as New Contemporaries (1988) Ltd. The exhibition was relaunched at the ICA in 1989.

which was preoccupied with breaking down (rather than fortifying) the limits of conventional mediums, both 'mixing' the arts and developing entirely new forms of practice: from Dada, Duchamp and Surrealism to Fluxus and the wide array of 'postformalist' event- and concept-based practices of the 1960s. This is a transmedia tradition that long predates recent acknowledgements of art's 'postmedium' condition. From its standpoint, the so-called canonical arts (painting and sculpture, in particular, but also more recent arts, like photography and video, when construed as mediums) represent an extremely limited set of ways of making art. Rather than the arts (plural, but finite), art in the generic singular defines the artistic field here, which is open to an infinite multiplicity of material forms of practices. But by what criteria then is it to be judged? Nowadays, the term 'contemporary art' generally refers to practices located within this open field, in so far as the continuation of the canonical arts, in their canonical forms, lacks contemporaneity by virtue of its insulation from other forms of social experience.

In the face of the crisis of the framework of critical judgement brought about by the inadequacy of formalist modernism to contemporary art, three main trends are discernible. First, a flight from judgement *per se*, in favour of an expansion of purely descriptive modes: a prohibition on judgements of 'quality'. Second, a retreat to general aesthetic criteria ('taste'), usually of a Humean rather than a Kantian kind (a historically established 'standard of taste', rather than a transcendental universality of judgement's form). This is often mixed in with residues of formalist modernism, and it frequently takes the form of a rhetorical retreat to the pure, ineffable singularity of the artwork. As such, it is the polar opposite of the first, discursive mode. Finally, there is the *de facto* emergence of the contemporary as an independent critical criterion.

Two things may be said about the type of critical judgement at stake in this third response. The first concerns its peculiar, but philosophically familiar, logical structure; the second, the varying breadths of the worlds encompassed by different judgements of contemporaneity. In the first case, judgements of contemporaneity seem to have the same logical structure of subjective universality as Kant's pure aesthetic, reflective judgements of taste. That is to say, the form of universality taken by a judgement of contemporaneity is that described by Kant as the 'strange *demand*' that others, universally, assent. Universality is not empirically achieved; rather, it sets the framework for the structure and character of a dispute, a dispute over universality. This is why the German philosopher Hannah Arendt saw in Kant's notion of aesthetic judgement the basis for a concept of political judgement. This leads to my second point, which is that 'the contemporary' is the site of what is ultimately a political conflict over definitions of the present. And one of the things at stake in that conflict is the breadth of the world encompassed by the different times brought together by different works of art, or what we might call the communicative range of their different definitions of the present. In the social space projected by its sharing of time, each work of contemporary art delineates the outline of a world. Be it a landscape painting of the Bangladeshi countryside, a high-definition photographic portrait, video footage of a workers' boarding house in Korea in the 1960s (repeated eight times, with sequential narrative variation) or film of a naked skateboarder – each work claims a particular shared present, and thereby makes a claim on you.

Look beneath the label. With which of these works do you a share a time and a world? And why? What claims does each make on you and your sense of the present? What is the politics of these claims?

Peter Osborne is the author of *The Politics of Time* (Verso, 1995; 2011), *Conceptual Art* (Phaidon, 2002) and *Marx* (Granta, 2005). *Anywhere or Not at All*, his new book on the philosophy of contemporary art, will be published by Verso in 2012.

10 Marie Angeletti	54 Ian Marshall
12 Cornelia Baltes	56 Georgina McNamara
14 Joshua Bilton	58 Sophie Neury
16 Sarah Brown	62 Rasmus Nilausen
18 Savinder Bual	66 Nick Nowicki
20 David Buckley	68 Marco Palmieri
24 Leah Capaldi	70 Selma Parlour
26 Alicja Dobrucka	72 Peles Empire
28 Tomas Downes	76 George Petrou
30 Katie Goodwin	78 Yelena Popova
32 Kate Groobey	80 Jessica Sarah Rinland
34 Noel Hensey	82 Anne Kathrin Schuhmann
36 Anna Ilsley	84 Dagmar Schurrer
38 Kim Kielhofner	86 Alison Stolwood
40 Minae Kim	88 Jonathan Trayte
42 Se-jin Kim	90 Poppy Whatmore
44 Sui Kim	94 David Ben White
46 Ute Klein	98 Lisa Wilkens
50 Hyewon Kwon	100 Samuel Williams
52 Hyun Woo Lee	102 Rafal Zawistowski

Marie Angeletti

Vivid, luminescent, precious, delicate, enticing,
yet inaccessible, detached. Marie Angeletti's
seductive photographs are assemblages of images
from our subconscious that draw one in, but also
create a deliberate distance.

Winter's Egg #1 2010
C-type print, 102 × 76 cm

Lights #1 2010
C-type print, 102 × 76 cm

Cornelia Baltes

The smallest observations and interferences conveyed through touchingly slight gestures, colours and rearrangements. Photographs as digital paintings that capture both daily life and the essence of an image whilst simultaneously obscuring it.

Untitled (house) 2010
Giclée print, 45 × 60 cm

Untitled (bird) 2010
Giclée print, 45 × 60 cm

Joshua Bilton

I am half in love with your tepee. It reminds me of what was once intended. In those days, the landscape was the world. The mind could not find a place outside of it. The wooden part is the outdoors is the indoors becoming part of me.

Post (diptych) 2010
black and white fibre-based prints, 35 × 29 cm

Sarah Brown

A flock of seagulls.

A flock of seagulls circling overhead in Alfred Hitchcock's film *The Birds*.

The anxiety and uncertainty in mundane life is apparent in Sarah Brown's drawings and begs the question: how much is real and how much is imagined?

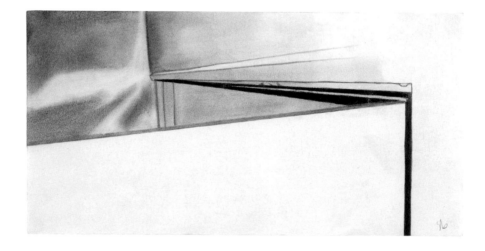

Is it a secret? 2010
pencil on paper, 15 × 29 cm

Entering into the Unknown 2010
pencil on paper, 30 × 30 cm

Train 2009
video, 2 sec (looped), (original photograph courtesy of Pete Hackney)

Savinder Bual

A steam engine superimposed on itself twenty
times or so in layers, vanishing in strobic flashes
to reveal the one behind, slightly larger, then
larger, then larger. Looped. Superimposed too
is the flickering sound of a mechanical projector
mixed in with – is it? – the whir of a computer
fan. Seen in such meagre frequency, the engine
doesn't pull in or roll or glide or chug or chuff in,
but stutters towards us as if geared by a trembling
finger over a cursor key.

Och, over a hundred years of moving pictures
and still, even in this elegant rendering of an
early cinematic paradigm, it's amazing how easily
tricked we are.

David Buckley

Much looks tabletop-made and pitted with fingers –
like most things that come to rest upon tables, come
to think of it.

In front of me I have a handbag radio, a telephone,
two framed pictures of windmills and a small icon
painted (not badly, I see now, but economically) on
stained pine, which is then rubbed down with gum.
There's an orchid with leaves like Alsatian tongues
begging, but it never flowers; nothing is bigger
than a fist, or a fist and a wrist. There is absolute
equilibrium between them, with no one rising
above the other, save for the phone, and then
only in volume. I have toyed with inserting a piece
of a folded cereal box between its bells.

What am I trying to say?

Without trying terribly hard, I can choose to
completely ignore these things. It all depends on
how much I can withstand their griminess, how
much they remind me of my living here.

The Rule 2010
acrylic on paper, marble, steel, 130 × 35 × 40 cm

We are, as usual 2010
cast iron, 180 × 50 × 40 cm

Hard Feelings 2011
cast bronze, chipboard, acrylic paint, foam rubber, 120 × 32 × 25 cm

Leah Capaldi

Alice jumping down the rabbit hole into Wonderland:
Leah Capaldi's work echoes this immediacy, while
constantly challenging ideas of comfort and propriety,
leaving the viewer seduced, baffled, uncomfortable
and overwhelmed. It is difficult to discern who is Alice
– the artist or the viewer. Maybe both.

Home 2010
C-type print, 14 × 10 cm

Alicja Dobrucka

Less concerned with specific events than conveying
the emotions that result from personal tragedies
and obsessions. A highly intuitive practice of
observing and capturing metaphorical associations,
which are finally determined through the editing
process. Sense, rather than story; moving flawlessly
between intimacy and detachment.

From the series: I like you, I like you a lot 2008–10
C-type prints, 30×30 cm

Tomas Downes

A little edge might give these structures a point to
pivot on, a hinge from which to swing like a screen
door. Or it might be a handle to yank, pulling the wall
clear from its skirting. These minor elevations afford
a shadow gap, a little depth and another cold space
– cold only because they allow so much to pass
through: colour and air and dust and hair in single
strands, framed yet spilling from one hollow shape
to another. As so many margins do, they promise
productivity, room for a certain scribbled distillation
of knowledge, some illumination.

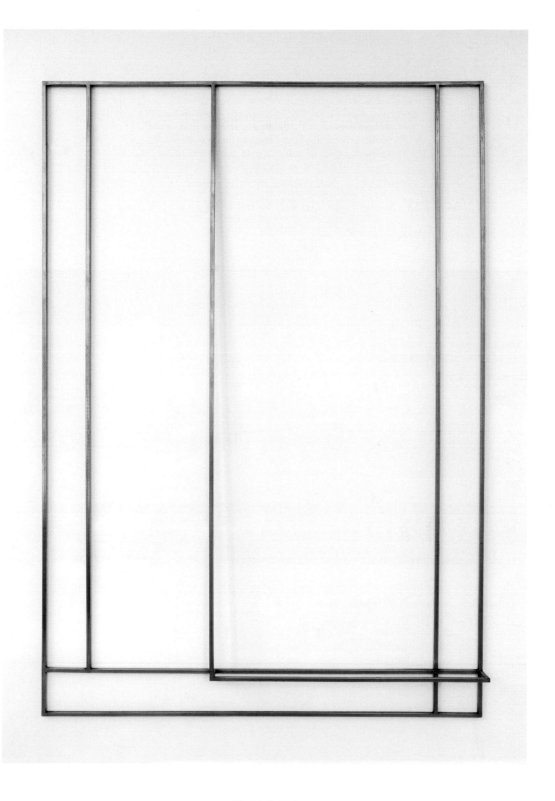

Untitled 2011
mild steel, 203 × 139 cm

Katie Goodwin

Usually overlooked and hidden cinematic moments
are revealed through a reprocessing of waste footage
gleaned from the 'cutting room floor'. Previous work
on feature films very much informs Katie's mainly
moving image practice. Light, vapour and dust are
recurring subjects.

Silent Landscape 2010
HD video, 3 min

Kate Groobey

Is that genitalia?

Never mind, he's not a criminal. He just wants
to chew a pathetic stick of spearminty gum every
so often.

What are the questions she asks herself from
this position in the world?

I tell them they have to look like children. Root out
importance. Find implications. Using my left hand
to pull the fabric away from my body, I read aloud
the label: 'Virgin lycra'.

Ask large questions, maybe. Why something and
not nothing? Why legs not particles? Why try to
describe it?

Bob's Trajectory 2011
oil on canvas, 30 × 25 cm

Massless Rod 2011
oil on canvas, 30 × 25 cm

Noel Hensey

In Morrissey font. 'Cause this is how sentiment
is rendered prophetic: true if in gawky capitals
and overwrought exclamation marks. In fire
escapes where piss concentrates into sticky
streaks and smells of gap years. These doors,
the saloon, this shot: a triad of hermetic space.
Observe: Death is here!

It's a zippy alignment. A wonderful synchronism
of captioned life in connotations of warm and cool
greys. We can imagine – I can imagine – her listening
to Kate Bush's, *This Woman's Work*; the pathos
wrapped up in plump reverb, Swilling, and barely
escaping the brilliant seal of the car doors. 'Give me
this moment back', she sings, blonde, staring ahead,
oblivious and observed from without.

Death is Here 2009
C-type print on aluminium, 42 × 60 cm

Anna Ilsley

'All this, Wilhelm, leaves me silent.'

So was it a do-I-need-a-jumper kind of day?
A sense of foreboding in the modern sunset.

'Like a hurricane', he said, 'the blocky colours
hurl over you and are no reassurance.'

It was a good place to start a relationship. Plot
potentials. Impossible to avoid stepping into.
Difficult to straddle one position.

'Yes', I said, 'like someone is coming to get me.'

'! – Shh – the air is thick with it! Something is
trying to lead you inwards, round cloaked pollards.
There might be somewhere to go or there might
not be.'

The Ghosts in the Back Garden 2010
oil on canvas, 130 × 200 cm

Bangladesh 2009
oil on canvas, 150 × 200 cm

Kim Kielhofner

Nothing smells of anything, nothing takes shape
or feels weighty or wet. Her words might as well
have been conjured from glances around the room:
peas and brown food. Crumbs, croissant, foot,
sock, skier. Smear, anchor, bed sheets. Baubles,
bubble-berry, blueberries and red jelly.

The sound of Hitchcock's *Marnie* dribbling in.
Marnie: a thief, mistrustful of men, fearful of thunder
and the colour red, Bleeding, seeping through the
calico and slowly turning green pillows brown.

Getting Marnie Out of the House 2010
video, 3 min 47 sec

Minae Kim

A site-responsive structure that can feign support
for disregarded architectural gaps, or that can stand
alone as a sculpture. Connecting geographically
and historically different spaces whilst mimicking the
essential characteristics of utilitarian objects. Is this
a physically useless assemblage or a paradoxically
useful visual prop?

A Structure to Maintain the Correct Distance Between Two Pillars 2010
wood, wheels, 160 × 245 × 76 cm

Se-jin Kim

'Early in the morning factory whistle blows,
Man rises from bed and puts on his clothes,
Man takes his lunch, walks out in the morning light,
It's the working, the working, just the working life.'
(Bruce Springsteen, *Factory*, 1978)

The quotidian journey of mind-numbing repetition,
the alienation between a worker and his work, and
drudgery that scrubs the personality are some of
the themes referenced in Se-jin Kim's films.

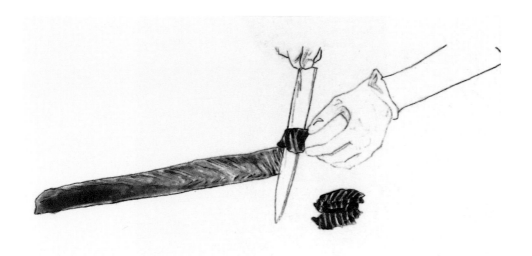

Hanna-Set 2011
multi-channel video, drawing images (looped), 1 min 1 sec

The Place I Like Best in the World is the Kitchen 2009
oil on canvas, 100 × 60 cm

Sui Kim

Deliberately avoiding the surreal or radical, these works are sourced from observations of contemporary life that somehow filter subconsciously into painting through a performative process akin to that of a dancer or a musician. A method of abstraction that happily sits outside of human language systems.

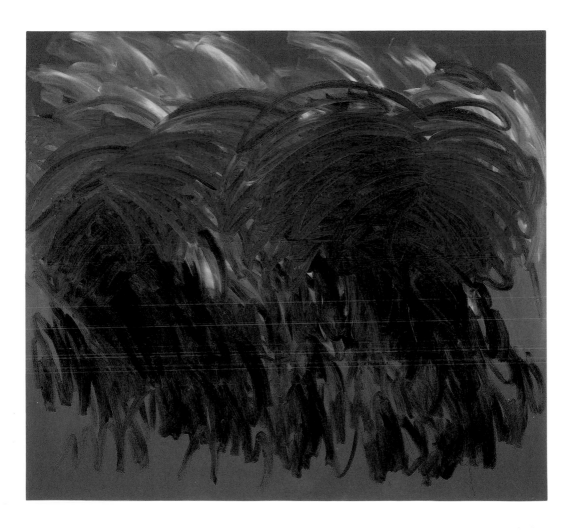

Tropical Dream 1 2011
oil on canvas, 170 × 190 cm

Ute Klein

Resonance braid. A humming weave. Responsive
weave. A good response. To meet with. To meet
with a positive response. To meet with a weave-y
response, a braided response. To chime together
amidst anachronistic soft furnishings and interlace.

A nose in the pit! Why not? And fingers burning
with pooling blood as they grip each other, pinch
each other, breathe in each other, their shampoo
and antiperspirant, lavender and laundered cotton.
The smell of his ear, her palm. Forgivable breath.

All cream cloth and coils of hair, though the twist
of a cat's tail on a pillow, there. The deficiencies
of a body and cuddling: awkward and uneconomic.

Whose spiralling limbs are these that we long
to lop off?

Resonanzgeflechte – leibhafter Raum
(Resonant Entanglements – Bodily Space) Resonanzgeflecht #9 2009
lightjet C-type print on dibond, 35 × 36 cm

Resonanzgeflechte – leibhafter Raum
(Resonant Entanglements – Bodily Space) Resonanzgeflecht #7 2009
lightjet C-type print on dibond, 35 × 36 cm

Resonanzgeflechte – leibhafter Raum
(Resonant Entanglements – Bodily Space) Resonanzgeflecht #8 2009
lightjet C-type print on dibond, 35 × 36 cm

Hyewon Kwon

History, or perhaps historical exclusion, as a discursive site, emphasises the omissions in a government's portrayal of events. Reawakening our perception of past realities with the suggestion that 'official' historical representations may have replaced our collective memory, both critiquing established modes of representation and seeking out new ways of writing history.

17 times of I hate this job. 2011
video, 48 sec (looped)

Hyun Woo Lee

Goodbye. You can take this as my notice.

For too long, I've been passing through one of those
periods in which significance is found only in dullness.
I don't know what I need. I need to get out of these
wet clothes and into a dry martini.

Plan B: become less obvious. I've been told I'm good
with children. More than that, I'm great to have around
in a tragedy: I take control, show spunk and affirmation.

Let's enjoy these aimless days while we can. All hell
will not break loose. Everything is linked. Everything
and nothing to be accurate.

Ian Marshall

Raw camera footage of a car bomb exploding
in the streets of Iraq.

A spectacular series of explosions as Gotham
General Hospital is blown to bits at the click
of a button, while the maniacal Joker – dressed
as a nurse – hobbles away.

Ian Marshall choreographs sequences of explosions
taken from popular media but completely removed
from their original context, to create a seemingly
banal yet ultimately cathartic visual cacophony.

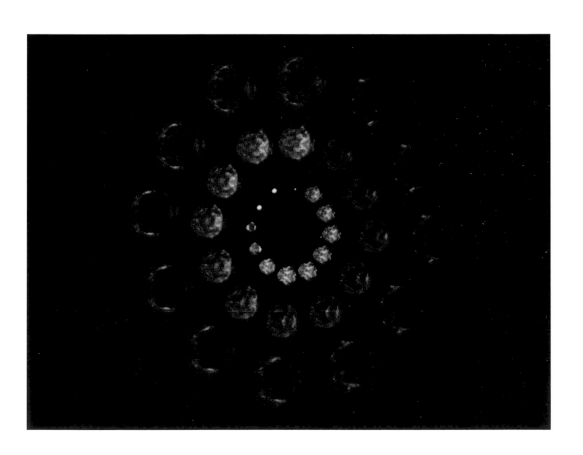

Berkeley Blooms 2011
cinematic projection, 4 min

Georgina McNamara

Thomas Pynchon, the famous yet obstinately
reclusive author, making his first public appearance
on an episode of *The Simpsons* as himself; with
a brown paper bag on his head.

An absurd and awkward look at human vulnerabilities,
Georgina McNamara's photographs bring forth
the constant tension between the parts of ourselves
we hide and those we choose to reveal.

Untitled (after Baldessari) 2010
C-type prints (2 of 7), 31 × 121 cm

Scene 2010
C-type print, 81 × 54 cm

Sophie Neury

The artist as active observer, who borrows the fieldwork methodology of the anthropologist. Examining the spatial articulations of objects and the way they can create new associations through metaphoric and symbolic systems. Immersion in an everyday environment such as the gymnasium, opens up an engagement with such objects, which are transformed and disrupted from their original function. Photography as a visual tool that supports and completes fragmented memories of spaces and which documents the tactile specificities of material encounters.

Untitled 1 (from the series De Arte Gymnastica) 2011
digital C-type print, 60 × 45 cm

Untitled 2 (from the series De Arte Gymnastica) 2011
digital C-type print, 60 × 45 cm

Untitled 3 (from the series De Arte Gymnastica) 2011
digital C-type print, 60 × 45 cm

Rasmus Nilausen

A diamond can be up to three billion years old.

A diamond was believed to ward off poison, insanity and inchoate fears, and to bring good fortune and victory to anyone who wore it on their left hand.

A diamond, like a painting, can be a forgery.

A diamond is the universal symbol of wealth, power and romance.

A Diamond is Forever.

Rasmus Nilausen shines a light on the process that informs the value we bestow upon objects.

The Sancy 2011
oil on linen, 81 × 65 cm

The Florentine 2011
oil on linen, 65 × 54 cm

The Dresden Green 2011
oil on linen, 65 × 54 cm

Nick Nowicki

They are made of bristles bound together, like
people. Nobody before had worked with such
big brushes.

Elsewhere, we are sitting in a place where everyone
looks familiar, waiting for the Heimlich manoeuvre.
I feel sad for people and the odd parts we play in
our narratives.

What are people? Do women wear box-pleat skirts
and embroidered cardies? Are men in donkey
jackets? What is the relevance of donkeys?

Woops! A drop of acrylic ink hits the surface.
Intensity sharpens to a triangle. I'm too scared
to look – the empty space, the way it nearly falls
off at the corners.

Hunting Ground 2010
acrylic on canvas, 190 × 270 cm

Marco Palmieri

The New Yorker (2001). A woman to her doctor:
'I think the dosage needs adjusting. I'm not nearly
as happy as the people in the ads.'

Marco's paintings illustrate with wry humour images
of urbane leisure, consumerism and 'high' culture.

Belsito 2010
oil on canvas, 160 × 110 cm

Our time Sir, is vile and anti-philosophical 2010
oil on canvas, 160 × 110 cm

Looks Like a Plan 2010
oil on linen, 76 × 61 cm

Selma Parlour

If modernist painting is opaque painting, what does it mean to bring depth to the grid? Form and space are interrogated here, colour activating surface texture. But where is the mark? These works blend the hard edge with the ethereal. Illusionistic Minimalism.

Room 2010
oil on linen, 150 × 163 cm

Peles Empire

You get these swathes of pattern, hand-smoothed swatches slathered in oil and dipped in pools, woven inlays and CMYK tartan, and women in stiff costumes of bowed wood and bent iron, crimping across rucked-up rooms and stumbling down their chequerboard floors, a range of false peaks rising up in curls, mirrored infinities embedded in ceilings and walls, '3D to 2D to 3D to 2D and back to 3D', analogue to digital, shifting, from one chamber to the next, the room tone wooo-ing, Woooooooo ...

A trick of the light; a trick of a charge-coupled device and electronic pulses.

Disco I 2011
digital print on paper, 70 × 50 cm

Disco III 2011
digital print on paper, 70 × 50 cm

Disco VI 2011
digital print on paper, 70 × 50 cm

George Petrou

Shall I do the cutting? I shall offer to you first. And
will you return my good manners and take the smaller
portion? If you do, I'll memorialise you in the stars,
o sister, and though light-years widely separated, we'll
spin enough for our twin image to come out, levelled
out and outlined in the sky, easily.

Remember Dad with his thumbs pulling apart a
prawn's thorax and head, sooking at her burlywood
brains – THUP – and too, her trillion eggs, a boon!
Clagging between her glassine legs? In the dump-bowl
beside, do you remember thinking how many were
once sisters?

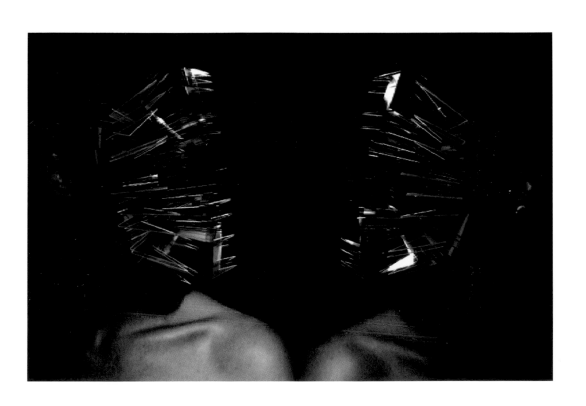

When we split in two 2011
video, 12 min 40 sec

UNNAMED 2011
video, 10 min

Yelena Popova

We gain understanding of the world through its
materiality and we evolve with the forces of nature.
Evolution is a tricky word, like progress. Both imply
some kind of positive growth, but also something
less healthy, like the accumulation of a disease.
Natural selection is only 'better' for certain species,
as is the good old modernist idea of a brighter future
for humankind. A secret nuclear town in Russia,
built on a peninsular and surrounded by lakes with
a military force that patrolled its borders, was an
ideal place for such a communist utopia to blossom.

Jessica Sarah Rinland

Break the news gently to my mother: I've realised
why the trousers are missing.

'Do not advance the action according to a plan',
she advised. 'Meanwhile here is a quick and
attractive garnish, suitable for any sea food.'

Whoa! Bodies! The responsibility of having one
was to occupy me on and off for an unspecified
period. Would somebody please initiate a deep
chest massage with soothing Vicks VapoRub?

Before I departed by skateboard, she parcelled
up the cutlery, adding: 'Distance is like the future.'

'When it comes to feeling and looking good', I called
after her, 'the breeze is all that matters.'

The Big Fish Theory 2009
16mm film, 4min

Nulepsy 2010
16 mm film, 8 min

Anne Kathrin Schuhmann

Hey! We don't wear expressions indoors around here.
Leave it in the area where the light sheen takes over.

Eyes. I've always been a fan of eyes, absolutely
nothing to look forward to.

This is nice, by the way. You can tell from the surface.
When something is put forward to us, we don't want
unthinkable secrets.

That takes care of the overall facial part. No use
trying to escape it.

Eyes. They look the same as twenty-five years ago.
They are looking! They are looking! They can only
look or not look.

Toria (1–4) 2010
C-type prints, 70 × 55 cm each

Dagmar Schurrer

The disruption between photographic image, narrative structure and text, all the while questioning the formal conventions of screen composition within a seamless combination of personal and found footage. The screenplay is exposed, along with all its apparatus and associations.

Rewind 2010
single screen projection, 2 min 35 sec

Alison Stolwood

Robert Nash's *Wilderness and the American Mind* is a cultural and philosophical examination of the evolution of the American concept of wilderness and conservation.

David Attenborough's stunning, insightful and path-breaking television series – *Life on Earth*.

Alison Stolwood's photographic animation explores how technology has impacted on our relationship with the natural world, and our understanding of the cyclical nature of time.

Wasp Nest 2010
photographic animation, 1 min 1 sec (looped)

Jonathan Trayte

I get pewter poured in the snow. Or a petrified
tree-trunk. A fictional natural history, one where
the alligators' eyes are all googly as they emerge
from the mires all swaddled in foil, and into the
jungly green of Lyme Bay.

What if we were to buff this one up,
this giant garden-find
this pig-rustled truffle
this queen nut
this elephant knee
this molten bottle bank
this sun-ruined Easter
this deventricularised beefheart?

What would it reveal in its gin translucency?

And what if we were to slice it and take a look at
its cross-section? I dare it would show its rings,
such is its visage of wholeness.

In the Presence of Nature 2011
gold-plated bronze, 23 × 48 × 30 cm

The Kiss 2011
painted bronze, 65 × 30 × 30 cm

Poppy Whatmore

Droog's Do hit chair: 'With the hammer provided
and your own resources you shape the metal box
into whatever you choose it to be. After a few minutes
or hours of hard work you become the co-designer
of Do hit.'

Poppy Whatmore's deconstructed and reconfigured
works address issues of individuality in our
contemporary consumerist society: how can
an art object evoke personal social history?

Cocked Leg 2009
hinged table leg levering the fourth leg of an assembled table, 75 × 180 × 80 cm

Flatpack 2010
deconstructed found wooden chair presented on the wall, 120 × 50 × 10 cm

I don't come prepared 2010
deconstructed chair frame with coloured gloss paint on wall, 60 × 120 × 20 cm

93

Painting Pavilion 1 2011
Giclée print, 50 × 33 cm

David Ben White

You might say we've got it all. Check out the lighting.

Come right in. Find a chair. Make yourself at home.
If I'm not mistaken, you're already in the room,
already seated.

Where?

You're here to avoid situations. Rooms are full of
situations – the utopian values of Esperanto, the
possibilities of a shared 'international style'. People.

We get lost looking. Here is where the wall was;
the suggestion of curtains.

Meanwhile the inevitable painting has slipped
in, along with a sense of failed promise: the
conversations I never had with my grandmother.
She thought chairs were largely demeaning
and moronic.

Painting Pavilion 2 (front) 2011
Giclée print, 50 × 33 cm

Painting Pavilion 2 (back) 2011
Giclée print, 50 × 33 cm

Lisa Wilkens

An investigation into the oldest genre of them
all and its enduring limitations and possibilities in
contemporary art. The image here is a product of
analysis: reconsidering the relationship between the
portrait and the perception of oneself. It conforms to
a formal understanding of portraiture but contradicts
the conceptual aspect. A portrait that does not portray.

Prevented Portrait: Myself 2011
lithograph on paper, 84 × 60 cm

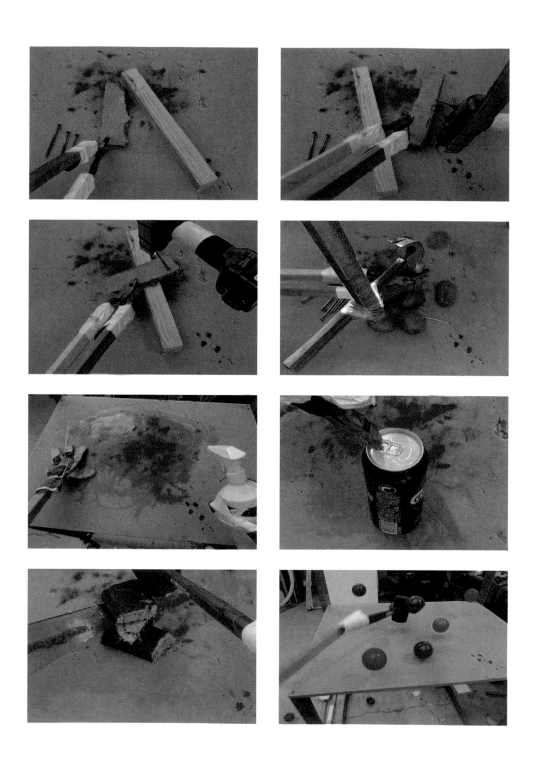

We are the Robots 2010
video, 6 min 15 sec

Samuel Williams

Lately, we've been banging long nails into baking
potatoes, fingering Swiss rolls, wondering whether
there's a way into this Carling Black Label. We cut
things up, bring evidence. It's getting out of hand.
What happens when we turn towards tongues,
for example?

The more you practice, the less likely something
is to happen. We have the most solid basis mixed
with something lesser.

Will people be glad they came, dug down into
primary foundations, poked closely into the basic
state of grains?

Transient pleasures, drastic measures. Might as
well not pick up the pieces.

Rafal Zawistowski

I wanted this man to be on my side. He had access
to _____ . He seemed no more than the apron of a face,
a way of looking.

He had the veneer of a ladies' man in the smash-up
of his career. A man or a desolate landscape?
A trampled-on forest. Yet still strangely attractive.
Death overwhelms even mediocrity.

JEEZ. Why must it always end this way?

'The face is the only avant-garde we have', I reply.
'And the name. Good name. Promotable.'

Jesus Christ 2011
encaustic on board, 150 × 100 cm

Artists' biographies

Marie Angeletti

b.1984 Marseille, France

2009–11   MA Photography, Royal College of Art, London
2007   MA Communication Arts, New York Institute of Technology

Recent Exhibitions

2011   Leica Prize, University of Applied Sciences Art Gallery, Bielefeld
2010   *Show 39*, Humble Art Foundation, New York
2008   *Foto8 Summershow*, HOST Gallery, London

Cornelia Baltes

b.1978, Mönchengladbach, Germany

2009–11   MFA Painting, Slade School of Fine Art, University College London
2003–06 Communication Design, Folkwang University of the Arts Essen, Germany
2000–03 Communication Design, University of Wuppertal, Germany

Recent Exhibitions

Solo
2010   *The Great Loop Forward*, Tank Gallery, London

Group
2010   John Moores Painting Prize, Walker Art Gallery, Liverpool
          Exhibitionism, Eastwing 9, The Courtauld Institute of Art, Somerset House, London
2008   *3 in 1*, Kunsthaus Essen, Germany
          Grosse Kunstausstellung, Museum Kunst Palast, Düsseldorf, Germany
2007   *Love Stories*, GAM – Galerie am Museum, Essen, Germany

Awards

2010   John Moores Painting Prize (finalist)
2009–11   Schüler-Stiftung Scholarship, Wuppertal
2006–08 Start-up Studio at Kunsthaus Essen e.V.
2006   Pentiment Academy Scholarship, Hamburg

Joshua Bilton

b.1983, Kings Langley, Hertfordshire

2008–10 MA Photography, Royal College of Art, London
2004–07 BA Photography, London College of Communication, University of the Arts London

Recent Exhibitions

2011 *International Departure: Gate 11*, Sant'Agostino Hospital, Modena, Italy
The Woodmill Studio Artists Group Show, London
2010 *The House of the Nobleman*, Boswall House, London

Awards

2010 Worshipful Company Painter-Stainers Award, UK

Sarah Brown

b.1989, Sheffield, Yorkshire

2009–11 BA Creative Art Practice, Sheffield Hallam University
2007–09 BTEC Higher National Diploma in Fine Art with Illustration, Hillsborough College, Sheffield
2005–07 BTEC National Diploma in Fine Art, Hillsborough College, Sheffield

Recent Exhibitions

2010 *Valise*, Sheffield Institute of Arts Gallery, Sheffield

Savinder Bual

b.1976, Hitchin, Hertfordshire

2008–10 MA Photography, Royal College of Art, London
1995–98 BA Painting, Winchester School of Art

Recent Exhibitions

2011 *The Woodmill Studio Artists Group Show*, London
2010 *Smoke & Mirrors*, Lightwell Gallery, University of Oklahoma
The Morouge Room, The Hospital Club, London
RE:animate, Oriel Davies Gallery, Newtown, Wales
2009 *Hal Silver*, The Russian Club Gallery, London

Awards and Residencies

2010 Escalator Retreat 6, Wysing Arts Centre, Cambridge
RE:animate, Student Category, Oriel Davies Gallery (2nd prize)

David Buckley

b.1980, Dublin

2008–10 MA Sculpture, Royal College of Art, London
2002–05 BA Fine Art, Goldsmiths, University of London

Recent Exhibitions

Solo
2011 *Your Affectionate Friend*, LimaZulu, London
2006 *Voyages*, Tou Vindu, Tou Scene, Stavanger, Norway

Group
2010 *State of the Newly Incarnate Soul*, Hidde van Seggelen, London
2009 *Over and Out*, Münster Ausstellunghalle, Münster, Germany
Sculpture Exhibition, Bank of America, London

Awards and Residencies

2011 Royal British Society of Sculptors, Bursary Award
2010 Remet Sculpture Award, Royal College of Art, London
2009 Cité Internationale des Arts, RCA Studio, Paris
2007 SÍM Residency, Reykjavík, Iceland
Scottish Sculpture Workshop Residency, Aberdeenshire, Scotland

Leah Capaldi

b.1985, Chertsey, Surrey

2008–10 MA Sculpture, Royal College of Art, London
2004–07 BA Sculpture, University of Brighton

Recent Exhibitions

2010 *EXPOSURE 2010*, Parasol Unit, London
Testing Ground: Live, 176/Zabludowicz Collection, London

Awards

2011 Catlin Art Prize (finalist)
2010 Parasol Unit EXPOSURE Award, London
2009 Stanley Picker Bursary, London

Alicja Dobrucka

b.1985, Kowary, Poland

2008–10 MA Fine Art Photography, London College of Communication, University of the Arts London
2005–06 BA Photography, FAMU, Prague
2004–07 BA Media Culture and Communications, University of Greenwich, London

Recent Exhibitions

Solo
2010 *I like you, I like you a lot*, Kiállítás Előtt Galéria, Tűzraktér Arts Center, Budapest

Group
2011 Sortiri Prize Exhibition, Galleria Guri Madhi, Korçë, Albania
2010 Hereford Photography Festival, Hereford
Fresh Faced and Wild Eyed, The Photographers' Gallery, London

Awards

2011 Bar Tur Award (shortlisted)
Sortiri Prize, France
2010 Deutsche Bank Fine Art Award in Photography, UK

Tomas Downes

b.1986, Birmingham, West Midlands

2008–11 PG Dip Fine Art, Royal Academy Schools, London
2005–08 BA Fine Art, Chelsea College of Art & Design, London

Recent Exhibitions

2011 *Young London*, V22 Workspace, London
2010 *Vicissitude,* Kabin Collection, London
Tomas Downes/Alexander Wolff, Peles Empire, London

Katie Goodwin

b.1979, St Albans, Hertfordshire

2010–11 MA Fine Art, Wimbledon School of Art,
         University of the Arts London
1998–01 BA Fine Art and Art History, Goldsmiths,
         University of London

Recent Exhibitions

2011 *Students, Paupers, Patients*, LSE, London
2010 *CLASH AND CONVERGE*, Camberwell
      Space, Camberwell School of Art, London

Kate Groobey

b.1979, Leeds, Yorkshire

2008–10 MA Painting, Royal College of Art, London
1997–00 BA Fine Art, Ruskin School of Drawing and
         Fine Art, University of Oxford

Recent Exhibitions

2010 *Newspeak: British Art Now Part 2*, Saatchi
      Gallery, London
      *Mare Street Biennale 2010: Unfeasibility
      Study*, Mare Street Biennale, London

Awards

2008 Stanley Smith Scholarship, Royal College
      of Art, London

Noel Hensey

b.1977, Dublin

2009–10 MA Fine Art, Chelsea College of Art &
         Design, University of the Arts London
2008–09 PG Dip Fine Art, Chelsea College of Art
         & Design, University of the Arts London
1995–00 BSc Technology with Design, University
         of Ulster, Northern Ireland

Recent Exhibitions

Solo
2008 *Sick*, Pallas Contemporary Projects,
      Dublin, Ireland

Group
2011 *Minor Domestic Interventions*,
      38b Peckham Rye, London
2010 *Q-Art London Presents II*, APT Gallery,
      London

Awards and Residencies

2011 Kildare County Council Emerging Visual
      Artists Solo Exhibition Award
      Red Mansion Art Prize (shortlisted)
2010 Chelsea Arts Club Trust Special Projects
      Award, London
2009 Kala Institute Residency, Berkeley, USA

Anna Ilsley

b.1982, Hitchin, Hertfordshire

2009–11 PG Dip, Prince's Drawing School, London
2003–06 BA Fine Art, Brighton University

Recent Exhibitions

2005 *Black Market*, Municipal Market, Brighton

Awards and Residencies

2010 Artist in Residence, International Institute
      of Fine Arts (IIFA), India
      Windsor and Newton Drawing Prize

Kim Kielhofner

b.1982, Richmond, Virginia, USA

2009–10	MA Fine Art, Central Saint Martins College of Art and Design, University of the Arts London
2004–07	BFA Studio Arts, Concordia University, Montreal, Canada

Recent Exhibitions

2011	*Boule de Neige*, articule, Montreal Red Mansion Prize, Triangle Gallery, Chelsea College of Art & Design, London
2010	*If you don't like the road you are walking, start paving another one*, Core Gallery, London

Awards and Residencies

2010	Research and Creation Grant, Canada Council for the Arts Red Mansion Art Prize
2008	Research and Creation Grant, Canada Council for the Arts Experimental Television Center Residency, New York

Minae Kim

b.1981, Seoul

2009–11	MA Sculpture, Royal College of Art, London
2004–07	MFA Fine Art, Graduate School of Seoul National University
2000–04	BFA Sculpture, College of Fine Arts, Seoul National University

Recent Exhibitions

Solo

2008	*Anonymous Scenes*, Kwanhoon Gallery, Seoul

Group

2011	*Space Study*, Plateau, Samsung Museum of Art, Seoul
2010	*Future's Future's Future*, Korean Cultural Centre UK, London London Festival of Architecture, The Welcoming City, Jubilee Park, Canary Wharf, London *Embrace*, Edinburgh College of Art, Edinburgh

Awards

2008	National Endowment Fund for Culture and the Arts, Arts Council Korea
2007	JoongAng Fine Art Prize (2nd Prize)

Se-jin Kim

b.1971, Daejeon, South Korea

2010–12 MFA Fine Art Media, Slade School of
Fine Art, University College London
2001–05 MA Film and Television, School of Media,
Sogang University
1990–94 BFA Oriental Painting, School of Art,
Hongik University

Recent Exhibitions

2011 *Welcome to Media Space*, Gallery
Jung-mi-so, Seoul
2009 *Media Archive Project 2009*, Arko Art
Center, Seoul
2008 *Asia Art Knots_Open Space_Art Cologne*,
Cologne
2007 *Soif d'aujourd'hui-Jeunes vidéastes
asiatiques*, Musée d'Art Moderne de
Saint-Etienne, Saint-Etienne, France

Awards and Residencies

2007 Go-yang National Art Studio by National
Museum of Contemporary Art, Korea
2006 Taipei Artist Village Residency, Taiwan
2005 Daum Prize, Park Geon-hi Art Foundation,
Seoul

Sui Kim

b.1983, Gyeonggi-do, South Korea

2010–12 MA Painting, Royal College of Art,
London
2006–09 BA Fine Art Painting, University of
Brighton

Recent Exhibitions

2009 *Hackney WickEd Art Festival*, Stour Space,
Fish Island, London
2008 *Painting*, Pall Mall Deposit, London

Awards

2009 Seoul National University Prize (finalist)

Ute Klein

b.1981, Bonn, Germany

2010–12 MA Fine Art Photography, Royal College
of Art, London
2003–09 Photography (Diploma), Folkwang
University of the Arts, Essen, Germany

Recent Exhibitions

2011 *Construct*, Folkestone Triennial Fringe,
Folkestone
Altitude + 1000, Festival de Photographie
de Montagne, Rossinière, Switzerland
2010 *gute aussichten 2009/2010*,
Deichtorhallen, Haus der Fotografie,
Hamburg, Germany
2009 Sélection 2009 Prix Voies Off, Festival
Voies Off des Rencontres d'Arles, France

Awards

2011 Munich Photography Award
2010 DAAD Fine Art Scholarship
2009 gute aussichten, Germany

Hyewon Kwon

b.1975, Seoul

2009–11 PhD Fine Art, University of Reading
2004–06 MFA Fine Art, Slade School of Fine Art,
University College London

Recent Exhibitions

Solo
2010 *Eight Men Lived in the Room*, Central
Gallery, Reading

Group
2011 *Screening 2011*, The Public, The West
Bromwich Arts Centre, West Midlands
2009 *Mullae Faction Project*, Future Text, Seoul
2007 *Single Shot*, Tate Britain, London
The Bigger Picture, Big Screen
Manchester, Manchester

Awards

2009 Seoul Foundation for Arts and Culture
(commission)
2007 Film & Video Umbrella and Film Council
UK (commission)

Hyun Woo Lee

b.1978, Seoul

2009–10 MA Fine Art, Chelsea College of Art &
Design, University of the Arts London
2001–04 BFA Painting, Kyungwon University,
Sungnam, Korea
1996–98 Associate Degree in Arts, Media Art,
Kaywon School of Art & Design, Uiwang,
Korea

Recent Exhibitions

Solo
2004 *1996–2004*, Alternative Space Loop,
Seoul

Group
2006 *Pull the Trigger*, BiBi Space, Daejeon,
Korea
2005 *Lyric Metaphor*, +Gallery, Nagoya, Japan
2003 *Energy*, Project Space Zip, Seoul
Door, SADI Space Gallery, Seoul

Ian Marshall

b.1982, Norwich, Norfolk

2010–12 MFA Fine Art, Goldsmiths, University
of London
2002–05 BA Fine Art, Birmingham Institute of
Art and Design

Georgina McNamara

b.1962, Woking, Surrey

2009–11 MA Fine Art, Central Saint Martins
College of Art and Design, University
of the Arts London
2007–08 PG Cert Photography, Central Saint
Martins College of Art and Design,
University of the Arts London
1995–01 BA Jewellery, Middlesex University
1980–83 BA History of Art, University of East
Anglia, Norwich

Recent Exhibitions

2010 Shoebox Photography Awards, Oblong
Gallery, London
RE:animate, Oriel Davies Gallery
Newtown, Wales
Some You Win, Some Deleuze, The
Factory, London
2009 *Creekside Open*, APT Gallery, London

Sophie Neury

b.1983, Moulins-sur-Allier, France

2009–11 MA Fine Art, Edinburgh College of Art
2007–09 BA Fine Art, Edinburgh College of Art
2003–07 DNAP, École Supérieure des Arts
Décoratifs de Strasbourg, France

Recent Exhibitions

2011 *Eleven*, Printworks, Talbot Rice Gallery,
Edinburgh
Salon Vert, Embassy Gallery, Edinburgh
2010 *Geometry of Soul*, John David Mooney
Foundation, Chicago

Awards and Residencies

2010 John David Mooney Foundation Residency,
Chicago
2009 Andrew Grant Bequest Major Award,
Edinburgh College of Art

Rasmus Nilausen

b.1980, Copenhagen, Denmark

2010–11 MA Fine Art, Chelsea College of Art &
Design, University of the Arts London
2006–10 BA Fine Art, University of Barcelona,
Spain

Recent Exhibitions

Solo
2011 *The Collection*, collaboration with
Nestor Delgago, Komando Kultura
Kontemporanea Barcelona
2010 Art & Design Barcelona, Barcelona
Projeccions 33, Cambra de la Propietat
Urbana, Barcelona

Group
2011 *Chelsea Salon Series*, The New Gallery,
London
2010 *S/T*, Galeria dels Àngels, Barcelona
2008 *BAC*, Centre de Cultura Contemporànea
Barcelona

Awards

2010 Nau Sud de l'Estruch, Spain
CoNCA, Consell Nacional de la Cultura
i de les Arts, Spain
Hielmstierne-Rosencroneske Stiftelse,
Denmark

Nick Nowicki

b.1968, Northampton, Northamptonshire

2010–12 MA Painting, Royal College of Art, London
2002–05 BA Fine Art, Central Saint Martins College
of Art and Design, University of the Arts
London

Recent Exhibitions

2010 *Desire is a Golden Carrot*, The Albion,
London
RCA Secret, Royal College of Art, London
6 × 4, Art Space Portsmouth, Southsea
Painting Show, 15 Howie Street, London
2006 *Curious New Terrain*, Nolia's Gallery,
London

Awards

2010 Ruby and Will George Trust, England

Marco Palmieri

b.1984, Tulsa, Oklahoma, USA

2008–11 PG Dip Fine Art, Royal Academy Schools,
London
2003–06 BA Fine Art, University for the Creative
Arts, Canterbury

Recent Exhibitions

Solo
2010 *The Black Crystals of the Night*, Margini
Arte Contemporanea, Massa, Italy

Group
2011 *The Private Life of Plants*, Peles Empire,
London
2009 *Bloomberg New Contemporaries*, Rochelle
School, London and Cornerhouse,
Manchester

Selma Parlour

b.1976, Johannesburg, South Africa

2008–12 PhD Art, Goldsmiths, University of London
2001–02 MFA, University of Reading
1995–98 BA Fine Art, De Montfort University,
Leicester

Recent Exhibitions

2007 Celeste Art Prize, London and Edinburgh
2006 National Open Art Exhibition, Chichester
2002 *Bench*, Tardis International, London

Awards

2007 Celeste Art Prize (finalist)
1999–01 AHRB Professional Practice Masters
Award

Peles Empire
(Katharina Stoever, Barbara Wolff)

founded 2005, Frankfurt, Germany

2006–10 PG Dip Fine Art, Royal Academy Schools,
London
2000–06 Staatliche Hochschule für Bildende
Künste, Frankfurt, Germany
2005–06 Student Exchange (Stoever), Slade School
of Fine Art, University College London
2002–03 Student Exchange (Wolff), Slade School
of Fine Art, University College London

Recent Exhibitions

Solo
2011 *Carmen Sylva*, Sierra Metro, Edinburgh

Group
2009 *Space Revised*, Geselleschaft für aktuelle
Kunst, Bremen, Germany
Transformation, Deutsche Bank, London

Awards

2010 Hessische Kulturstiftung, Travel Grant
2009 Deutsche Bank Award
2007 MAK Schindler Scholarship, Los Angeles

George Petrou

b.1981, Paphos, Cyprus

2009–11 MA Photography, Royal College of Art,
London
2005–08 BA Fine Art, Chelsea College of Art &
Design, University of the Arts London

Recent Exhibitions

Solo
2008 *Self Portraits*, Maus Hábitos-Espaço
de intervenção Cultural, Porto, Portugal

Group
2011 *Shorts*, Modern Art Oxford, Oxford
2010 *Album*, Wolstenholme Creative Space,
Independents, Liverpool Biennial
Z-Time, Era Gallery, Moscow International
Biennale for Young Art

Yelena Popova

b.1978, Ural, Russia

2009–11 MA Painting, Royal College of Art, London
2006–07 PG Dip Fine Art, Byam Shaw School of
Art, University of the Arts London
1995–00 BA Set Design and Technology, MHAT,
Moscow

Recent Exhibitions

Solo
2010 *UNNAMED*, Wallner Gallery, Lakeside
Arts Centre, Nottingham

Group
2011 *Keep Floors and Passages Clear*,
White Columns, New York
Tracing Shadows in the Dark, Blyth
Gallery, London
Salt, RU Arts Gallery, Moscow
International Biennale for Young Art
Z-Time, Era Foundation, Moscow
International Biennale for Young Art
2010 *Oasis*, Bury St Edmunds Gallery

Awards

2011 Red Mansion Prize

Jessica Sarah Rinland

b.1987, Esher, Surrey

2008–10 BA Fine Art, Central Saint Martins College
of Art and Design, University of the Arts
London
2007–08 Foundation in Art and Design, Central
Saint Martins College of Art and Design,
University of the Arts London

Recent Exhibitions and Screenings

2011 *Nulepsy*, 49th Ann Arbor Film Festival,
Michigan, USA
2010 *Nulepsy*, 48th New York Film Festival
Run Bird Run, Cannes Short Film Corner
The Big Fish Theory, 7th London Short
Film Festival
2008 *A Great Day to Loose Him To Adeline*,
Camden Arts Centre, London
To Rock and To Cease, Curzon Cinema
with Jonas Mekas, London

Residencies

2011 Virtue and Industry Residency, Picture
This, Bristol

Anne Kathrin Schuhmann

b.1982, Gera, Germany

2009–11 MA Fine Art Photography, Royal College
of Art, London
2002–08 Diploma Photography at University of
Applied Sciences, Bielefeld, Germany

Recent Exhibitions

2010 *Album*, Wolstenholme Space, Liverpool
2009 *Jeune Création*, Le 104, Paris
2008 *BAC*, Centre de Cultura Contemporànea
Barcelona

Awards and Residencies

2010 Artist in Residence at School of Visual
Arts, New York
2009 Man Group Photography Prize (3rd prize)
2007 Prix Leica (shortlisted)

Dagmar Schurrer

b.1980, Vöcklabruck, Austria

2007–11 BA Fine Art, Central Saint Martins College of Art and Design, University of the Arts London

Recent Exhibitions

2010 *Gesamtkunstwerk 2012*, Hackney Rose, London
2009 *CHÂTEAU D'IF*, Shoreditch Town Hall, London
2009.75, Lewisham Arthouse, London

Awards

2011 William Barry Trust Scholarship, London

Alison Stolwood

b.1983, Colchester, Essex

2009–11 MA Photography, University of Brighton
2002–05 BA Photography, Falmouth College of Art

Recent Exhibitions

2010 *UKX10*, Lotte Avenuel, Seoul
2009 *Lost in Transit*, Impressions Gallery, Bradford and Vyner Street Gallery, London

Awards

2011 University of Brighton Springboard Award

Jonathan Trayte

b.1980, Huddersfield, Yorkshire

2007–10 PG Dip Fine Art, Royal Academy Schools, London
2001–04 BA Fine Art, University for the Creative Arts, Canterbury

Recent Exhibitions

Solo
2011 *In the Presence of Nature*, Canterbury Cathedral

Group
2010 *Franks-Suss Collection*, Saatchi Gallery, London
2009 *Bloomberg New Contemporaries*, Rochelle School, London and Cornerhouse, Manchester

Awards

2011 Land Securities Award
2010 Jealous Print Prize

Poppy Whatmore

b.1976, Oxford, Oxfordshire

2009–11 MFA Sculpture, Slade School of Fine Art, University College London
2008–09 PG Certificate of HE for Art and Design, Centre for Learning and Teaching Art and Design, University of the Arts London
2005–08 BA Sculpture, Camberwell College of Arts, University of the Arts London

Recent Exhibitions

Solo
2009 *Architectonic*, Tea's Me, London

Group
2009 *Belonging*, Earl's Court Festival, London
Art Projects Consultancy, Barnes, London
2008 *Ishihara*, Kube Gallery, Poole, Dorset

Awards and Residencies

2010 Heals Residency
Merz Barn, Residency
2009–11 Arts and Humanities Research Award (AHRC)

David Ben White

b.1965, London

2010–12 MA Fine Art, Chelsea College of Art &
Design, University of the Arts London
2009–10 PG Dip Fine Art, Chelsea College of Art
& Design, University of the Arts London
2003–06 BA Fine Art, Central Saint Martins College
of Art and Design, University of the Arts
London

Recent Exhibitions

Solo
2010 *Painting Pavilion*, (And/Or Gallery),
London
The Atom Age Parts 1 & 2, Studio 1.1,
London

Group
2011 *How Could Everybody Be So Wrong*,
(And/Or Gallery), London
2010 *Misfits*, Galerie DS, Belgium
2008 *Working Space 2*, Lucy Mackintosh
Gallery, Lausanne, Switzerland
Working Space, The Arts Gallery, London

Lisa Wilkens

b.1978, Berlin

2010–11 MA Printmaking, Camberwell College of
Arts, University of the Arts London
2001–05 Diploma in Design / Scientific Illustration,
University of the Arts, Zurich

Recent Exhibitions

Solo
2010 *Discarded*, Changing Spaces, Cambridge
2009 *intersections parts 1 & 2*, Changing
Spaces, Cambridge

Group
2010 *omnium gatherum*, Warehouse Studio,
Cambridge
2006 *haut, falten, beutel*, Monia Herbst, Berlin
Tatorte, Schriftbild, Berlin

Samuel Williams

b.1980, Oxford, Oxfordshire

2009–11 MA Sculpture, Royal College of Art,
London
2000–04 BA Critical Fine Art Practice, University
of Brighton

Recent Exhibitions

Solo
2011 *INSTRUCTIONS*, Inova, Milwaukee, USA
2010 *Serpentine New Music Action*, Cafe Oto,
London

Group
2010 Group Show, Kyoto Art Center, Japan

Awards

2010 Exchange, Kyoto City University of Art,
Japan

Rafal Zawistowski

b.1981, Warsaw

2010–11 MA Fine Art, Wimbledon College of Art,
University of the Arts London
2002–06 BA Fine Art, Ontario College of Art,
Toronto, Canada

Recent Exhibitions

2011 *Futura Bold / Futura Oblique*, The Nunnery,
London
Fly Tipping, The Centre for Drawing,
Wimbledon College of Art, London
CCW Salon, New Gallery, London

Residencies

2004–05 Florence Residency, Ontario College of
Art and Design

Bloomberg New Contemporaries is open to all final year undergraduates and current postgraduates of Fine Art at UK colleges and those artists who graduated in the year 2010.

Selectors' biographies

Pablo Bronstein (b.1977, Buenos Aires) lives and works in London. He completed a BA Fine Art at the Slade School of Fine Art (2001) and an MA Visual Arts at Goldsmiths, University of London (2004). Solo exhibitions include *Sketches for Regency Living* at Institute of Contemporary Arts, London (2011); *Alternate Colour Scheme for Sewage Works*, Kunstal Charlottenborg, Copenhagen (2011); *Garden à La Mode*, Tate Britain (2010); *Pablo Bronstein at the Met*, Metropolitan Museum of Art, New York (2009); and Städtische Galerie im Lenbachhaus und Kunstbau, Munich (2007). Significant group shows include *Move: Choreographing You*, Hayward Gallery, London (2010); Manifesta 8, Murcia, Spain (2010); PERFORMA 07, New York (2007); and Tate Triennial, London (2006).

Sarah Jones (b.1959, London) lives and works in London. She studied for a BA Fine Art and Contemporary Dance (1981) and MA Fine Art (1996) at Goldsmiths, University of London. Solo exhibitions include The National Media Museum, Bradford (2007); Huis Marseille Foundation for Photography, Amsterdam (2000); Museum Folkwang Essen, Germany (1999); and Museum Reina Sofia, Madrid (1999). Significant group shows include *Heroines*, Museo Thyssen-Bornemisza and Fondacion Caja, Madrid; *A Sense of Perspective*, Tate Liverpool; *Dutch Still Life*, Peabody Essex Museum, Massachusetts, USA (all 2011); *Portraits*, Bloomberg SPACE, London (2008); *Street and Studio: An Urban History of Photography*, Tate Modern, London and Museum Folkwang, Essen, Germany (2008); *Northern Lights: Reflecting with Images*, Galleria Civica, Modena, Italy (2007).

Michael Raedecker (b.1963, Amsterdam) lives and works in London. He studied BA Fashion Design at Gerrit Rietveld Academie in Amsterdam (1990) and BA Fine Art at Rijksakademie van Beeldende Kunsten, Amsterdam (1994) and MA Fine Art at Goldsmiths, University of London (1997). Solo exhibitions include *line-up*, Camden Arts Centre, London (2009); *instinction*, Centro Nazionale per le Arte Contemporaneo, Rome and Museum für Gegenwartskunst, Basel (2002); *extract*, Van Abbe Museum, Eindhoven, Netherlands (1999). Significant group shows include *Changing Times – New Worlds*, Gemeentemuseum Den Haag, The Hague (2010); *Painting Now!*, Kunsthal Rotterdam (2007); and *Painting at the Edge of the World*, Walker Art Center, Minneapolis, USA (2001). He was nominated for the Turner Prize in 2000.

Published by New Contemporaries [1988] Ltd
on the occasion of the exhibition:

Bloomberg New Contemporaries 2011

S1 Artspace and Site Gallery, Sheffield
23 September – 5 November 2011
www.s1artspace.org
www.sitegallery.org

Institute of Contemporary Arts, London
23 November 2011 – 15 January 2012
www.ica.org

Bloomberg New Contemporaries
Rochelle School
Arnold Circus
London E2 7ES
+44 (0)20 7033 1990
www.newcontemporaries.org.uk

Artist commentaries written by
Patrick Coyle: pp. 12, 26, 31, 40, 45, 50, 58,
71, 79, 85, 98; Siôn Parkinson: pp. 19, 20, 28,
34, 39, 46, 72, 76, 88; Chinmoyi Patel: pp. 10, 16,
24, 42, 54, 56, 62, 68, 86, 90; Heather Phillipson:
pp. 15, 32, 36, 53, 66, 80, 82, 95, 101, 102

ISBN: 978-0-9566133-1-8

Bloomberg New Contemporaries would like
to thank: Ed Atkins, Sarah Boris, Tyler Bright
Hilton, Lizzie Carey-Thomas, Mike Carney, C'Art,
Cornerhouse, Stephen Draycott, Geoff Fazan,
Lex Fenwick, Luke Gottelier, Jeanine Griffin, Anna
Gritz, Katie Haines, Trevor Hall, Louise Hutchinson,
John Jones, Des Lawrence, Sheila Lawson, Julie
Lomax, Doug McFarlane, David Micheaud, James
Moores, Fraser Muggeridge, Gregor Muir, Emily
Musgrave, Eleanor Nairne, Sarah Newitt, Margred
Pryce, Jemma Read, Red Leader, Tom Scutt, Pippa
Shaw, Laura Sillars, Lois Stonock, Emma-Jayne
Taylor, Karen Turner, Jeanette Ward, Helen Wewiora,
and Matt Williams.

Catalogue edited by
Eileen Daly and Rebecca Heald

Editorial Assistant
Sandra Mahon

Photography by
Andy Keate, photographers and video artists
Photograph p.118 Simone Koch

Designed by
Fraser Muggeridge studio

Printed by
EBS – Editoriale Bortolazzi-Stei

sponsored by

in partnership with

Cover: Peles Empire, *Disco VI*, 2011 (detail)
digital print on paper, 70 × 50 cm